# RAYMOND JACK TYLER

# DUCKS AS PETS

First published by Raymond Jack Tyler 2024

Copyright © 2024 by Raymond Jack Tyler

All rights reserved. No part of this publication may be reproduced, stored or transmitted in any form or by any means, electronic, mechanical, photocopying, recording, scanning, or otherwise without written permission from the publisher. It is illegal to copy this book, post it to a website, or distribute it by any other means without permission.

First edition

This book was professionally typeset on Reedsy.
Find out more at reedsy.com

# Contents

1 Chapter 1    1
  INTRODUCTION TO DUCKS AS PETS    1
    The Charm Of Ducks    1
    Types Of Pet Ducks    3
    Legal Considerations And Local Regulations    5

2 Chapter 2    8
  CHOOSING THE RIGHT BREED FOR YOU    8
    Breed Personalities And Behaviors    8
    Egg Laying, Meat, Or Companion?    10
    Size And Space Requirements    12

3 Chapter 3    15
  SETTING UP A SAFE HOME FOR YOUR DUCKS    15
    Indoor Vs. Outdoor Housing    15
    Coop Design And Essential Features    17
    Safety And Predators    19

4 Chapter 4    22
  FEEDING YOUR DUCKS FOR OPTIMAL HEALTH    22
    Nutritional Needs Of Ducks    22
    Foods To Avoid    24
    Feeding Schedules And Portions    26

5 Chapter 5    28
  MANAGING DUCK HEALTH AND HYGIENE    28
    Common Health Issues And Prevention    28
    Bathing, Preening, And Grooming    30
    First Aid And Emergency Care    32

6 Chapter 6    35

ENRICHMENT AND SOCIALIZATION FOR HAPPY DUCKS ............ 35
   Creating A Stimulating Environment ............ 35
   Duck-To-Duck Socialization ............ 37
   Human-Duck Bonding And Interaction ............ 39
7 Chapter 7 ............ 42
  BREEDING AND RAISING DUCKLINGS ............ 42
   Understanding Duck Breeding Behavior ............ 42
   Incubating Eggs Vs. Natural Hatching ............ 44
   Duckling Care And Growth Stages ............ 46
8 Chapter 8 ............ 49
  TRAINING YOUR DUCK ............ 49
   Basic Commands And Tricks ............ 49
   Potty Training Ducks ............ 51
   Reward-Based Training ............ 53
9 Chapter 9 ............ 56
  SEASONAL CARE AND ADAPTING TO WEATHER ............ 56
   Summer Care Tips ............ 56
   Winter Care Tips ............ 58
   Adapting To Changing Seasons ............ 61
10 Chapter 10 ............ 64
  COMMON QUESTIONS AND TROUBLESHOOTING ............ 64
   Managing Noise And Behavioral Issues ............ 64
   Dealing With Messes And Cleaning Routines ............ 66

# 1

# Chapter 1

## INTRODUCTION TO DUCKS AS PETS

### The Charm Of Ducks

Ducks can be surprisingly wonderful pets for people who have the right setup. Compared to some other animals, ducks are relatively low-maintenance, although they still need special care to stay happy and healthy. One of the best things about ducks is their friendly personalities. Ducks are social animals that like to spend time with others, including their human caretakers. Many duck owners find that their ducks follow them around like loyal companions, similar to how a dog might act. This kind of behavior makes ducks a fun choice for people looking for a unique pet that offers companionship.

Ducks also have a playful side. They love water and enjoy splashing around, which can be a lot of fun for both the ducks and their owners, especially if there's a pond or even a small kiddie pool in the yard. Ducks are naturally curious and enjoy exploring their surroundings, which keeps things interesting for everyone involved. Watching ducks play, waddle around, or splash in the water can be entertaining and relaxing. Just seeing a group of ducks interact with each other can bring joy to anyone's day.

### The Unique Joys of Having Ducks as Pets

Ducks offer a different kind of companionship compared to pets like dogs or cats. While they may not be as openly affectionate as some other animals, they show their appreciation in their own ways. For example, many ducks will follow their owners around or sit nearby while resting. Some duck breeds are especially friendly and may even enjoy being petted or held. Ducks also recognize people who care for them and often greet them with happy quacks and friendly behavior.

One of the unique joys of having ducks is their love for routine. Ducks do best when they have a daily schedule, and setting up a regular routine with them can be very rewarding. Feeding, cleaning, and interacting with ducks at the same times each day helps create a bond based on trust. Over time, ducks and their owners get used to each other's routines and enjoy spending time together.

Another interesting thing about ducks is the way they communicate. Ducks make different sounds to express their feelings or needs, and owners who spend enough time with them start to understand the different types of quacks. This kind of communication helps build a strong, unique bond between ducks and their owners.

### Making Sure Ducks Are a Good Fit for You

Although ducks can be great pets, they aren't the right choice for everyone. Ducks need outdoor space, ideally with access to water like a small pool or pond, because they enjoy swimming and playing in water. They also need shelter that can protect them from predators and harsh weather. It's important to make sure you have a secure, safe area where they can roam and feel comfortable.

Ducks also need companionship, as they are social animals. It's best to have more than one duck, so they don't feel lonely. If you're considering getting ducks, you'll need to be prepared to care for at least two ducks, as a single duck might get stressed or unhappy on its own.

Ducks need regular care, including feeding and cleaning, so they're not a "set it and forget it" kind of pet. But for people who are willing to spend the time, ducks can bring a lot of joy. They have unique personalities, they're full of energy, and they're great companions.

# CHAPTER 1

Understanding the Rewards of Having Ducks as Pets

The companionship of ducks is special because it's both subtle and deeply rewarding. Ducks may not jump into your lap like a dog or purr like a cat, but they show affection in their own gentle ways. When a duck waddles over to you or quietly sits nearby, it's a sign of trust and comfort. Many duck owners find that the calm presence of ducks brings a sense of peace and connection.

## Types Of Pet Ducks

When thinking about keeping ducks as pets, it's important to understand the difference between domestic ducks and wild ducks. Domestic ducks are bred specifically to live with people, while wild ducks are better suited to life in nature. Knowing the difference will help you choose the right type of duck and ensure it has the best care.

**Domestic Ducks vs. Wild Ducks**

Domestic Ducks are raised in farms or homes for human care and have been bred over many generations to get along well with people. These ducks are typically easier to handle, calmer, and less likely to get stressed around humans. They enjoy interacting with their owners and can adapt to living in backyards or on small farms.

On the other hand, Wild Ducks are meant to live in nature. They are not used to human contact and can become stressed or scared by being kept as pets. Wild ducks also have special needs that are hard to meet in a home setting. They are usually protected by law, so it is illegal in many places to capture or keep wild ducks as pets. Removing wild ducks from their natural habitats can harm the environment and the ducks themselves, so it's better to admire them from afar in the wild.

For those who want a pet duck, domestic breeds are the better choice. These ducks are comfortable living with humans and thrive in environments where they are cared for properly. Domestic ducks are friendly, manageable, and well-suited for living in a home or a small farm.

**Popular Domestic Duck Breeds for Beginners**

If you're new to keeping ducks, there are several breeds that are especially good for beginners. These ducks are known for their friendly personalities, easy care, and ability to adapt to different environments. Here are a few popular breeds:

1. Pekin Ducks: Pekin ducks are one of the most common breeds for first-time duck owners. They have soft, white feathers and are known for their calm, friendly nature. Pekins are easy to take care of, making them a great choice for those new to duck-keeping. They enjoy human interaction and are good for people who want a relaxed and approachable pet. Pekins adapt well to a variety of environments, whether it's a small backyard or a larger farm.

2. Rouen Ducks: Rouens look a lot like Mallards, but they are larger and have a calmer temperament. These ducks are less likely to fly away, which makes them easier to keep in a backyard. Rouens are gentle and social ducks that enjoy spending time with humans. They are good for families or anyone who wants a calm, easygoing duck that enjoys human company. Their size and docile nature make them suitable for a more laid-back environment.

3. Indian Runner Ducks: Indian Runner ducks are famous for their tall, upright posture and energetic behavior. They are very active and curious, so they love to explore their surroundings. These ducks are great for people who want a more energetic pet. They are excellent foragers, meaning they enjoy searching for food and are very entertaining to watch. However, because they are so active, they might require more space and mental stimulation than some other breeds. If you enjoy watching a lively and inquisitive duck, the Indian Runner is a good choice.

**Choosing the Right Duck for You**

The breed of duck you choose will depend on your lifestyle and the kind of experience you want to have with your pet. Some ducks are more affectionate and enjoy spending time with people, while others are more independent but still fun to care for. When choosing a breed, consider factors like how much time you can spend with your duck, how much space you have, and how much energy you want from your pet.

For example, if you have a busy lifestyle and want a calm, easy-to-care-for pet, a Pekin or Rouen duck might be the best option. If you enjoy watching an active and curious pet that explores a lot, an Indian Runner might be a good match. No matter which breed you choose, domestic ducks can make wonderful pets with the right care.

## Legal Considerations And Local Regulations

Before getting a pet duck, it's important to make sure you're following the rules and laws in your area. Different places have different rules about keeping ducks, and you'll want to check the local regulations to avoid any problems.

**Zoning Laws and Permits**

In many cities or towns, there are zoning laws that set rules about what kinds of animals can be kept in residential areas. Some areas don't allow any kind of farm animals, including ducks, within city limits. In other places, there might be restrictions on the number of ducks you can keep, or they may only allow certain breeds. For example, you may be allowed to have a couple of ducks in your backyard, but you might need a special permit to keep more, or to have ducks in certain areas of the city.

Before getting a duck, you should check with your local government or animal control office to make sure ducks are allowed in your area. If a permit is required, you may need to fill out an application and pay a fee. It's always better to check these regulations first to avoid any legal issues later.

**Wildlife Regulations and Wild Ducks**

It's also important to know that wild ducks are protected by laws in many places. Wildlife regulations protect ducks and other wild animals, so it's illegal to capture, keep, or keep wild ducks as pets in many areas. Wild ducks need to live in their natural habitats, and removing them from the wild can harm them and disrupt the local ecosystem. In some places, it is strictly prohibited to keep wild ducks as pets, and doing so can lead to fines or other legal trouble.

Instead of keeping wild ducks, it's a better idea to look into domestic breeds of ducks that are meant to live in a home or farm setting. Domestic ducks are bred to be friendly with people and can adapt to life in a backyard, whereas wild ducks are better off staying in the wild.

**Being a Responsible Duck Owner**

Owning a duck is a big responsibility. Ducks are social animals and need company, so it's recommended to have at least two ducks. If you keep only one, it might become lonely and stressed because ducks enjoy being with others. A pair of ducks will have each other to keep company, share food, and protect each other from danger.

Ducks also need plenty of space to move around, explore, and swim. They are happiest when they have access to water where they can bathe, swim, and play. A small kiddie pool or a pond is a good option for pet ducks. They also need an area where they can roam freely, forage for food, and feel safe. The space should be secure to protect them from predators like raccoons, foxes, or even neighborhood dogs.

Besides space, ducks require daily care. They need fresh food and clean water every day. Ducks are messy eaters, so you will need to clean their feeding area regularly to keep it sanitary. They also need shelter to protect them from bad weather, such as rain, snow, or extreme heat. A small duck house or a shed can provide this shelter, but it should be well-ventilated and easy to clean.

Ducks also require regular health checks. Like any pet, ducks need to be monitored for signs of illness, parasites, or injuries. It's a good idea to have a vet who specializes in birds or farm animals to check on your ducks from time to time to ensure they are healthy.

**Ethical Considerations**

Owning ducks isn't just about following the laws—it's also about understanding the ethical responsibilities involved. Ducks require time, attention, and effort, so before getting ducks, make sure you are ready to commit. They are not animals that can be left alone for long periods. If you travel often or work long hours, you may need to make arrangements for someone to care for your ducks when you're away.

In addition to daily care, it's important to keep their environment clean and safe. Ducks can easily get sick if their living space isn't kept clean, and it's your responsibility to make sure their home is well-maintained. You should also provide proper nutrition and make sure they have enough space to stay active and healthy.

Taking care of ducks is not just about giving them food and water. It's about creating a safe, comfortable environment where they can live happy

# CHAPTER 1

and healthy lives. This involves understanding their natural behaviors and needs and being prepared to give them the care they deserve.

# 2

# Chapter 2

## CHOOSING THE RIGHT BREED FOR YOU

### Breed Personalities And Behaviors

Just like other pets, ducks have different personalities and behaviors. Some ducks are very friendly and enjoy interacting with people, while others are more independent or shy. When choosing a pet duck, it's important to understand these differences to pick the breed that will fit best with your lifestyle and what you want from a pet.

**Differences in Temperament**

Different duck breeds have different temperaments, meaning their personalities can vary a lot. For example, Pekin ducks are well known for being friendly and calm. They are usually very gentle and enjoy being around people, making them a great choice for families, especially those with children. Pekins tend to be easygoing and approachable, which is a big reason why they are so popular as pets.

Rouen ducks, while still friendly, are a little more reserved than Pekins. They get along well with humans, but they are not quite as outgoing or affectionate. Rouens are still good companions but may not be as eager for attention as Pekins.

If you are looking for a more energetic and active duck, the Indian Runner might be the right choice. These ducks are lively, curious, and always on the move. They are known for their upright posture and fast, running style. Indian Runner ducks are perfect for people who want a more active pet that loves to explore.

On the other hand, Muscovy ducks are often more independent. While they can still bond with their owners, they tend to be less social and may not seek as much human interaction. Muscovies enjoy their own space more than other breeds, so they may not be the best choice if you're looking for a duck that loves to cuddle or follow you around.

Finally, Mallards, while beautiful, are wild ducks and are not typically kept as pets. They can be skittish around humans and might not be as docile as other domesticated breeds. If you're looking for a duck that is calm and friendly, Mallards may not be the best option, as they are more nervous and less likely to bond with people.

**Noise Levels**

Ducks can be noisy, and some breeds are louder than others. If you live in a suburban or urban area where noise might bother your neighbors, it's a good idea to choose a quieter breed. Muscovy ducks are one of the quieter breeds. Instead of quacking loudly like other ducks, they make softer noises such as whistles and trills. These sounds are not as disruptive as the quacking of other breeds, which might make Muscovies a better choice for people who want a less noisy duck.

On the other hand, breeds like Pekin ducks and Khaki Campbells are known for being quite vocal, especially during feeding times or when they're communicating with each other. Pekins, in particular, can be very loud, making a lot of noise when they are excited or want attention. If you don't mind the sound of quacking, these ducks can be a lot of fun, but if noise is a concern, you may want to choose a quieter breed.

**Activity Levels**

The activity level of a breed is another important factor to consider when choosing a pet duck. Indian Runner ducks are very active and full of energy. They love to explore and are often seen running around quickly. This makes them a fun and entertaining pet, but it also means they need a lot of space and stimulation. If you have a large yard or outdoor space for them to explore, Indian Runners will be a great choice.

In contrast, Pekin and Rouen ducks are more laid-back and enjoy a calmer environment. These ducks prefer leisurely walks around the yard and may not be as energetic as Indian Runners. If you live in a smaller space or don't have a large yard, these breeds might be a better fit. They are happy to waddle around in a more relaxed manner and don't require as much exercise as more active breeds.

Choosing the right breed also depends on how much space you have. If you have a big backyard or a pond for them to swim in, more active breeds like the Indian Runner will enjoy having plenty of room to move. But if you live in a smaller area or don't have as much space for your ducks to roam, it's better to choose a breed that doesn't need as much room, like the Pekin or Rouen.

## Egg Laying, Meat, Or Companion?

When you decide to get ducks, it's important to think about what you want from them. Are you interested in having ducks that lay eggs, produce meat, or just keep them as pets? Different breeds of ducks are better for different purposes, so understanding your goals will help you pick the best breed for your needs.

**Ducks for Egg Laying**

If you want ducks mainly for their eggs, you should choose breeds known for laying a lot of eggs. Khaki Campbell ducks are one of the best choices for egg production. They can lay between 250 and 300 eggs each year, making them a great option for people who want a steady supply of eggs. These ducks are active and like to forage, which helps them find food and stay healthy, making them perfect for laying lots of eggs.

Another breed that is excellent for egg production is the Indian Runner duck. Like Khaki Campbells, they also lay about 250-300 eggs per year. Indian Runners are known for being active and curious, and they make good foragers, which can help them lay eggs consistently.

Other good breeds for laying eggs include the Welsh Harlequin and the Runner ducks. These breeds are also good at laying eggs regularly. However, if you're just looking for ducks to lay eggs for personal use, Pekin and Rouen ducks can still be good choices. They will not lay as many eggs as Khaki Campbells or Indian Runners, but they still produce a decent number each year.

**Ducks for Meat Production**

If your main interest in ducks is for meat, it's best to choose breeds that grow quickly and produce a lot of meat. Pekin ducks are a popular breed for meat production. They grow quickly and are known for having tender, flavorful meat. Pekins are large ducks, and they mature faster than many other breeds, making them a good choice if you want both eggs and meat.

Another breed raised for meat is the Muscovy duck. Muscovies are a little different from other ducks. They are more muscular and have leaner meat. Muscovy ducks are often chosen for their quality meat rather than their egg production, so they are a great option if you are focused mainly on meat.

While Rouen ducks are often raised for both eggs and meat, their meat yield is not as high as Pekins. However, Rouens still produce a good amount of meat and are considered high-quality ducks for meat production.

**Companion Ducks**

If you want ducks as pets or companions, there are certain breeds that are better suited for this purpose. Pekin ducks are a great choice for people who want friendly and easy-to-handle ducks. Pekins are known for being calm, gentle, and social, which makes them perfect for families or individuals looking for a pet. They are also one of the most popular duck breeds for pets due to their laid-back nature.

Rouen ducks are another good option if you want a companion duck. They are friendly and get along well with humans, though they are generally a bit more reserved than Pekins. If you want a duck that is calm and can bond with you, Rouens make a great choice.

Other breeds that are good as companion ducks include the Cayuga and Swedish ducks. These breeds are friendly and enjoy being around people, though they tend to be less active than some of the more energetic breeds like the Indian Runner. If you're looking for a duck that will enjoy your company but is less demanding, these breeds might be a good fit.

While ducks like the Indian Runner can also be kept as pets, they are very active and may not be as calm or easy to handle as breeds like Pekin or Rouen ducks. Indian Runners are perfect for people who want a more energetic and interactive duck, but they are not always as gentle or social as other companion breeds.

## Size And Space Requirements

When you decide to get ducks, it's important to think about how much space you have and how much room the ducks will need to stay healthy and happy. Different breeds of ducks require different amounts of space, so understanding the size of the ducks you want will help you plan their living space better.

**Larger Ducks Need More Space**

Larger breeds like Pekin and Rouen ducks require more space to live comfortably. These ducks are bigger and need plenty of room to roam around. They need a large yard or a big pond where they can stretch their legs, forage, and swim. Ducks are naturally curious and enjoy exploring their surroundings. If you only have a small yard, it might be harder to meet the needs of these larger breeds.

Pekin ducks, for example, are very friendly and enjoy interacting with people, but they need enough space to stay healthy. Without enough room, they may become stressed or unhappy. Rouen ducks, although a little less energetic than Pekins, are still large and require a spacious environment. If you plan to have more than one of these ducks, you will need to make sure there is enough space for them to move around freely and interact with each other.

**Smaller Ducks Need Less Space**

On the other hand, smaller breeds like Indian Runner and Call ducks need less space. These ducks are smaller in size, so they are a good option if you have a small yard or live in a more urban environment. While they still need space to roam, they won't require as much room as the larger breeds. Indian Runner ducks, for example, are known for their energy and love to run around, but they don't need a huge yard to do so. They can be kept in smaller spaces as long as they have room to move and play.

Call ducks are even smaller and are often kept in more compact spaces. They are a good choice for people with limited space, such as those who live in townhouses or have small backyards. However, even small ducks need a safe and secure environment where they can enjoy the outdoors.

**Shelter for Your Ducks**

In addition to space for roaming, ducks also need shelter. Ducks need a place to stay safe, especially when the weather is bad. Whether it's too hot, too cold, or rainy, a shelter will help protect them from the elements. You should provide a dry, clean, and safe place where your ducks can rest and sleep at night. This shelter can be as simple as a small coop or a larger barn, but it should be sturdy enough to protect your ducks from predators, like raccoons or foxes.

The size of the shelter depends on how many ducks you have. Larger ducks need bigger shelters, while smaller breeds can manage in a smaller space. Just make sure that the shelter is big enough for all your ducks to comfortably fit inside, especially if you are keeping them together. It should also have proper ventilation to keep the air fresh and to reduce moisture inside, which can lead to health problems.

**Pond or Water Access**

Ducks love water, so if you can, provide them with access to a pond or a kiddie pool. This is especially important for larger breeds like Pekin and Rouen ducks, as they enjoy swimming. Swimming helps them stay healthy and keeps them entertained. If you don't have a pond, a small pool in your backyard can be enough for smaller breeds like Indian Runners and Call ducks.

It's important to note that ducks will make a mess in water, so you'll need to make sure their pond or pool is kept clean. Dirty water can cause health problems for ducks, so you should change the water regularly or have a way to clean it.

**Feeding Your Ducks**

Feeding your ducks also depends on their size. Larger breeds like Pekins and Rouens need more food than smaller breeds like Indian Runners. You should plan your feeding budget based on the size of the ducks you are keeping. Ducks eat a variety of foods, including grains, vegetables, and special duck pellets. Make sure they have enough food and water every day. Ducks also need grit (small stones) to help them digest their food, so be sure to provide this as well.

# Chapter 3

## SETTING UP A SAFE HOME FOR YOUR DUCKS

### Indoor Vs. Outdoor Housing

When you get ducks, one of the first decisions you'll need to make is whether to keep them indoors or outdoors. Both options have their pros and cons, and the choice depends on factors like the space you have, the climate in your area, and how much time you want to spend caring for them.

**Outdoor Housing**

Outdoor housing is often the best option for ducks because it gives them plenty of space to roam, forage, and engage in natural behaviors, like swimming. Ducks enjoy being outside, where they can access fresh air, sunlight, and water. Having a pond, pool, or even a small kiddie pool is very beneficial for their well-being, as they love swimming and cleaning themselves in the water.

Outdoor housing also provides more room for ducks to explore and exercise, which is important for their physical and mental health. Ducks are very curious animals, and they enjoy wandering around their environment, looking for food, and interacting with other ducks. This helps keep them entertained and prevents boredom, which can lead to stress.

Another advantage of outdoor housing is that it's less messy than indoor housing. Ducks are naturally messy animals—they splash water, track mud, and make a lot of waste. In an outdoor setting, it's easier to manage the mess because the space is bigger and more open. If you have a large yard or property with a secure fence, outdoor housing is a great option.

However, outdoor housing also has some challenges. The most significant concern is keeping your ducks safe from predators. Wild animals like raccoons, foxes, and birds of prey can harm your ducks, so you need to make sure their outdoor housing is secure. This means building a strong, safe shelter for them and using a sturdy fence to protect them from predators.

Weather is another factor to consider when housing ducks outdoors. If you live in a place with harsh winters or extremely hot weather, you'll need to make sure your ducks have a safe and comfortable shelter to protect them from rain, snow, or high temperatures. Ducks need a dry, insulated place to sleep, especially in extreme weather conditions. They are hardy animals but still need shelter to stay healthy and safe.

**Indoor Housing**

Indoor housing can be a good option if you live in a small space or want to have more control over the environment your ducks live in. If you keep your ducks indoors, they can be housed in a large room, like a basement, garage, or a specially designed space. This setup helps protect them from predators and harsh weather, and it may be easier to monitor their health and cleanliness.

Some people even treat their indoor ducks like pets, allowing them to roam freely around the house, much like cats or dogs. If you want to bond closely with your ducks and enjoy their company inside your home, indoor housing could be a great choice. Ducks can form strong bonds with their owners, and keeping them indoors allows you to interact with them regularly.

However, indoor housing does come with some challenges. Ducks can be very messy, especially because they need water to drink, bathe, and clean themselves. This can create splashes and messes indoors, especially if they don't have a designated area for bathing. Their waste can also be smelly and harder to manage inside the house.

If you decide to keep ducks indoors, you need to make sure the space is large enough for them to move around comfortably. Ducks need room to spread their wings and walk around, so a small room might not be suitable. You also need to be prepared for frequent cleaning to keep their area sanitary and fresh.

Another important consideration is that ducks need access to sunlight and fresh air for good health. If ducks are kept indoors for long periods without exposure to natural light, they can develop health problems like vitamin D deficiency. To prevent this, you'll need to make sure they spend time outside each day, either in a safe outdoor enclosure or in a fenced yard, where they can enjoy the sunlight and get exercise.

## Coop Design And Essential Features

Whether you choose to house your ducks indoors or outdoors, having a well-designed coop is essential for their health and happiness. The coop is where your ducks will sleep, rest, and lay their eggs, so it must be secure, comfortable, and easy to clean. Here are the key features you should include when designing a coop for your ducks.

**Nesting Areas**

Ducks need a quiet and secure place to lay their eggs, so a nesting area is an important feature of any coop. Nesting boxes should be placed in a private, peaceful corner of the coop, away from the areas where ducks eat or rest. This gives the ducks the privacy they need to feel comfortable while laying their eggs. The boxes should be filled with clean straw, hay, or wood shavings. These materials provide a soft, comfortable surface for the ducks to rest on and make laying their eggs easier.

It's also important that the nesting boxes are easy to clean, but secure enough to protect the eggs from predators. In some areas, animals like raccoons or other birds may try to steal the eggs, so make sure the nesting boxes are well-secured and hard for predators to reach.

**Roosting Spaces**

While ducks don't roost like chickens, they still need a designated place to sleep at night. A roosting area should be spacious enough for all your ducks to rest comfortably without crowding. Some ducks prefer to sleep on the ground, while others enjoy a raised platform or perch. If you live in a colder climate, consider raising the roosts off the ground. This can help keep your ducks dry and warm, especially during the winter months.

When designing the roosting area, make sure the platforms or perches are wide and stable enough for the ducks to sleep without falling. Ducks are not great at gripping onto narrow surfaces, so it's important that the roosts are wide enough to keep them safe and comfortable. The ducks should be able to lie down without slipping or getting hurt.

**Cleaning Accessibility**

A clean living space is very important for the health of your ducks. Ducks can produce a lot of waste, and if their living area isn't cleaned regularly, it can quickly become dirty and unhygienic. To make cleaning easier, design the coop with materials that are easy to wipe down. Materials like concrete or wood with waterproof coatings are ideal because they don't absorb moisture or waste. Avoid using fabrics or carpets in the coop because these materials can soak up moisture and become difficult to clean.

The coop should also have good ventilation. Proper airflow helps to prevent odors, reduces moisture buildup, and keeps the air fresh, which is important for your ducks' health. Without proper ventilation, the coop can become damp, which can lead to respiratory issues or other health problems for the ducks.

One of the most important aspects of keeping the coop clean is removing duck waste regularly. Duck droppings can build up quickly, so it's essential to clean the coop often to avoid health problems like bacterial infections or respiratory issues. A good design should include removable trays or floors that can be easily hosed down or cleaned. This makes it much easier to clean the coop quickly and maintain a hygienic environment for your ducks.

Another useful feature to include is an area for storing food and water. Ducks need access to clean food and water at all times, and you should make sure that their feeding and drinking areas are easy to access and clean. Consider installing automatic feeders or waterers to make feeding more convenient and to reduce the amount of mess in the coop.

## CHAPTER 3

**Protection from the Elements and Predators**

In addition to making the coop easy to clean, you should make sure it's secure from predators. Ducks are vulnerable to wild animals like raccoons, foxes, or birds of prey, especially if they are left outside overnight. To protect your ducks, ensure that the coop has secure doors, windows, and fencing. The fencing should be tall and strong enough to prevent animals from getting in, and the doors should lock securely. If you keep ducks in an outdoor coop, make sure the shelter is insulated to protect them from harsh weather, such as rain, snow, or extreme heat.

## Safety And Predators

Keeping your ducks safe from predators is one of the most important things you need to think about when setting up their home. Ducks are vulnerable to many types of animals, including raccoons, foxes, coyotes, and birds of prey. To keep your ducks safe, you need to make sure their housing is secure and protected from these threats.

**Fencing Options**

A strong, secure fence is one of the best ways to protect your ducks from predators. The fence should be at least 4 feet high to prevent predators like foxes or coyotes from jumping or climbing over. If you have a larger property or live in an area with many wild animals, you may want to use even higher fencing to provide extra security.

To keep predators like raccoons from digging under the fence, bury the bottom of the fence a few inches into the ground. Raccoons are skilled at digging and can easily get under a low fence. By burying the bottom, you prevent them from sneaking in. For the material of the fence, wire mesh or welded wire is a great option. These materials are strong and durable, and they don't have gaps that predators can slip through. This will ensure that your ducks stay safely inside the fenced area.

Another important detail is to check the fence regularly to make sure it remains intact. Look for any gaps, loose wires, or areas where the fence may have been damaged, and fix them right away. A fence that's not well-maintained can create openings that predators can use to get to your ducks.

**Safe Housing Practices**

Along with a secure fence, it's important to make sure the duck coop is also safe and protected. The coop should have a solid door with a latch that's strong enough to prevent predators from opening it. Even if a predator can't break through the fence, a weak door or latch could still allow it to get inside the coop.

If you live in an area with a lot of wildlife or known predators, it's a good idea to reinforce the coop with additional protection. This might include adding extra wire mesh or hardware cloth around the coop, especially in areas where predators might try to get in, like around the door, windows, or any gaps in the walls. Hardware cloth is strong and provides a tight barrier that predators can't get through. Adding these extra layers of protection helps make sure the coop is as secure as possible.

Make sure the coop is always securely closed at night when your ducks are most vulnerable. Many predators, like raccoons and foxes, are active at night, so keeping the coop tightly shut after dark is essential to keep your ducks safe.

For extra protection, consider adding a roof to the coop. A roof will not only protect your ducks from the weather, but it will also keep out birds of prey like hawks and eagles. These birds can be a serious threat to smaller ducks, especially when they're outside during the day.

**Providing Shelter and Hiding Spots**

Ducks also need a safe, sheltered area where they can go if they feel threatened. Providing places where ducks can hide, such as sheltered corners, sheds, or structures with overhead cover, helps them feel secure. If ducks are able to quickly escape to a safe spot, they will be less stressed and have a better chance of staying calm if a predator is nearby.

Hiding areas can be simple, such as a small shelter or a pile of straw, that the ducks can run to when they need to escape. You should make sure that these shelters are secure, dry, and easy for the ducks to get to in case of danger. This adds another layer of protection and peace of mind for both you and your ducks.

It's also a good idea to train your ducks to recognize the safe areas and use

CHAPTER 3

them if needed. Ducks can learn where it's safe to hide, and over time they will understand which places to run to when they sense danger.

# 4

# Chapter 4

## FEEDING YOUR DUCKS FOR OPTIMAL HEALTH

### Nutritional Needs Of Ducks

Ducks, like all animals, need a balanced diet to stay healthy. Their diet should include three main types of nutrients: protein, fat, and carbohydrates. Each of these nutrients helps ducks stay strong, active, and healthy. Understanding these nutritional needs is important to ensure your ducks thrive.

**Protein**

Protein is very important for ducks because it helps them grow strong, build muscles, and lay eggs. Young ducks, or ducklings, need more protein than adult ducks. Ducklings should eat food with about 18-20% protein in their diet. Adult ducks, on the other hand, should eat food with 16-18% protein, depending on their age and activity level.

If you are raising ducks for egg production, protein is especially important. This nutrient is needed to make eggs, and without enough protein, egg production may decrease. You can give your ducks extra protein by offering them treats like mealworms, cooked eggs, or insects and worms they find while foraging. These are natural sources of protein that can complement their regular diet.

**Fat**

Fat is another important nutrient because it gives ducks energy to stay active and healthy. Ducks actually need more fat than chickens. For adult ducks, their feed should contain about 5-7% fat. This helps them maintain energy levels, especially if they are very active or live in colder climates.

To provide healthy fats, you can add foods like sunflower seeds, flaxseed, or fishmeal to their diet. However, it's important not to give them too much fat because it can cause obesity. Ducks that are overweight may face health problems like joint issues, and this can also reduce their egg production.

**Carbohydrates**

Carbohydrates are the main energy source for ducks. They get most of their carbs from grains like corn, oats, and wheat, which are commonly found in duck feed. Ducks also enjoy foraging for carbohydrates by eating grasses, seeds, and aquatic plants. These natural foods help them stay energized for their daily activities like swimming, walking, and exploring.

When feeding your ducks, it's important to make sure their diet has a good balance of protein, fat, and carbohydrates. Many commercial duck feeds are designed to meet all these needs, but you can also add extra grains or vegetables to supplement their diet and keep them healthy.

**Supplements and Treats for a Healthy Diet**

While ducks can get most of their nutrition from good-quality commercial feed, they also love extra treats and supplements. These can add variety to their diet and even offer health benefits. Some common treats and supplements include:

- Grains and Seeds: Ducks enjoy snacks like sunflower seeds, cracked corn, and oats. These can be given as treats or added to their feed in small amounts.
- Greens and Vegetables: Ducks like leafy greens such as spinach, lettuce, kale, and dandelion leaves. They also enjoy vegetables like peas, carrots, and cucumbers. Offering these fresh foods can provide extra vitamins and minerals.
- Calcium Supplements: If you have female ducks that are laying eggs, they need extra calcium for strong egg shells. You can give them crushed

oyster shell or crushed eggshells to help with this. Calcium is crucial for egg production and for keeping your ducks healthy.

• Grit: Ducks need grit to help with digestion. Grit is small stones or sand that ducks swallow, which helps break down food in their stomach. Ducks that free-range will usually find their own grit, but if they are kept in a contained area, you should provide it for them.

While these treats and supplements are great, it's important not to give them too much. Overfeeding treats can upset the balance of their diet and cause health problems. Make sure that their main feed provides all the essential nutrients, and only give treats in moderation to add variety to their meals.

## Foods To Avoid

Ducks are not very picky eaters, and they enjoy a wide variety of foods. However, there are certain foods that can be harmful or even toxic to them. It is essential to know what not to feed your ducks in order to keep them safe and healthy. Below are some common foods that should be avoided.

**Toxic Foods for Ducks**

1. Avocados Avocados contain a substance called persin, which is harmful to ducks. If ducks eat avocados, it can lead to serious health problems such as difficulty breathing, heart damage, or even death. It's best to avoid feeding your ducks any part of an avocado, including the flesh, skin, or pit.

2. Chocolate Chocolate is toxic to ducks because it contains a chemical called theobromine. This substance can cause major health issues, even if the ducks consume only a small amount. Symptoms of chocolate poisoning in ducks include vomiting, diarrhea, and seizures. Always keep chocolate and chocolate-based foods away from your ducks.

3. Onions and Garlic Onions and garlic are dangerous for ducks, especially in large quantities. They contain compounds that can damage ducks' red blood cells, which can lead to a condition called anemia. Anemia is when the body does not have enough healthy red blood cells, which can make the ducks weak and sick. It's important to avoid giving your ducks onions or garlic, whether they are raw, cooked, or in any processed form.

4. Citrus Fruits Citrus fruits like oranges, lemons, and grapefruits are not inherently harmful to ducks in small amounts. However, if ducks eat too much citrus fruit, it can cause digestive upset or interfere with calcium absorption. Calcium is essential for laying ducks to produce strong egg shells, so it's best to limit citrus fruits in their diet. Moderation is key if you decide to give them any citrus.

5. Raw Potatoes Raw potatoes, especially the green parts of the potato, contain a toxic substance called solanine. This compound can cause nausea, upset stomach, and in severe cases, even death if consumed in large amounts. To keep your ducks safe, never feed them raw potatoes. Cooked potatoes without any seasoning are safer, but they should still be offered in moderation.

6. Salt Ducks do not need a lot of salt in their diet. Too much salt can cause dehydration and kidney problems. Foods high in salt, like chips or processed snacks, should never be given to ducks. If ducks consume too much salty food, it can lead to serious health issues, so avoid adding salt to their diet or feeding them salty human foods.

**General Guidelines for Feeding Ducks**

While it's important to avoid the foods listed above, there are many healthy foods you can offer your ducks. Ducks love vegetables, grains, and specially formulated commercial duck feed, which provides most of the nutrients they need. You can feed ducks leafy greens like lettuce, spinach, and kale, as well as peas, corn, and other vegetables. Grains such as oats, barley, and cracked corn are also good for them.

Commercial duck feed is often designed to provide the right balance of protein, vitamins, and minerals for ducks, so it's a great option to make sure they are getting a complete diet.

**Safety First**

If you're ever unsure about a food or treat, it's always best to double-check whether it's safe for ducks. Avoid feeding them foods that are processed, salted, or contain harmful ingredients like sugar or artificial flavors. Instead, stick to natural, whole foods and fresh water. Ducks should always have access to clean, fresh water to help with digestion and overall health.

By being mindful of the foods you offer and avoiding harmful foods, you'll be helping your ducks live happy, healthy lives. Providing them with the right diet ensures they get the nutrition they need and prevents potential health problems down the line.

## Feeding Schedules And Portions

Ducks, like all animals, thrive on routine. Having a consistent feeding schedule is important for their health and happiness.

**Feeding Schedule**

Ducks should be fed at least twice a day. A good feeding schedule is in the morning and then again in the late afternoon or evening. This allows them to have enough food to keep their energy levels up throughout the day. It's important to remember that ducks need access to fresh water when they eat. Water helps them digest their food and stay hydrated, so always provide clean water whenever you feed them.

For adult ducks, the amount of food they need each day is around 1/4 to 1/2 pound (about 113 to 227 grams) of food. The exact amount depends on the size of the duck and how active they are. Ducks that are more active, like those that spend a lot of time swimming or foraging, may need slightly more food.

Ducklings, or baby ducks, have different needs. They are smaller and require less food, but they need to eat more often. Ducklings should be fed at least 3 to 4 times a day, and, like adult ducks, they need clean water available at all times. As they grow, you can start feeding them fewer times a day, and their portions will increase to match their growing needs.

**Portion Control**

While ducks love to eat, it's important not to overfeed them. Overfeeding can lead to obesity, which can cause health problems like joint pain, difficulty moving, and even reduced egg production. The key to keeping your ducks healthy is to provide the right portion sizes.

To make sure you're feeding your ducks the right amount, keep track of how much food you give them each day. Adjust their portions based on their weight and activity level. If they seem to be gaining too much weight, you can reduce the portions slightly. On the other hand, if they're very active and seem hungry all the time, you may need to give them a bit more food.

If you are feeding them commercial duck feed, many brands will provide guidelines on how much to feed based on the age and size of your ducks. These guidelines are a helpful starting point, but you can always adjust based on your ducks' individual needs. Be sure to check your ducks' weight and how much food they're leaving behind after meals to gauge if you're feeding them the right amount.

**Variety in Their Diet**

In addition to portion control, it's important to offer variety in your ducks' diet. Ducks love a mix of foods, and variety ensures they get all the nutrients they need to stay healthy. A good diet for ducks includes grains, vegetables, and protein-rich foods.

Common grains you can feed your ducks include corn, oats, and barley. Ducks also enjoy vegetables such as leafy greens like spinach, lettuce, and kale. You can also offer them peas, carrots, and cucumbers. Protein-rich foods like mealworms, earthworms, and cooked eggs can be offered as well.

Feeding your ducks a variety of foods keeps them interested in their meals and ensures they get a balanced diet. A variety of foods also helps provide the different vitamins, minerals, and nutrients that ducks need to stay healthy.

**Treats and Snacks**

Ducks enjoy treats, and these can be offered in moderation. Treats can add some fun to their diet, but they should not replace their regular meals. Some good treat options include small amounts of cracked corn, sunflower seeds, and even small pieces of fruit or vegetables. Be sure to avoid feeding them too many treats, as this can lead to an unbalanced diet.

Also, remember that treats should not make up more than 10% of their overall diet. The majority of their food should come from their regular duck feed or from fresh, nutritious grains and vegetables.

# Chapter 5

## MANAGING DUCK HEALTH AND HYGIENE

### Common Health Issues And Prevention

Ducks are generally strong and resilient animals, but like all pets, they can face health problems. Understanding the most common health issues that ducks experience and knowing how to prevent them is important to keep them healthy and happy. Some of the most common health issues include bumblefoot, respiratory infections, and parasites.

**Bumblefoot**

Bumblefoot is a common condition in ducks that affects their feet. It happens when their feet become swollen, infected, or even ulcerated. Bumblefoot is often caused by injury, poor hygiene, or standing on hard surfaces for too long. Ducks that spend a lot of time walking on rough surfaces, like concrete or wire flooring, are more likely to develop bumblefoot.

To prevent bumblefoot, make sure your ducks have soft bedding to walk on, like straw or wood shavings. If possible, avoid hard or rough surfaces in their living area. If they have to walk on hard ground, make sure there are areas where they can walk on softer surfaces. Keeping their living space clean is also important. Regularly clean the coop and your ducks' feet to prevent dirt and bacteria buildup. If you notice any swelling or infection on their feet, take action quickly. Early treatment can stop the condition from getting worse and causing more problems.

**Respiratory Infections**

Respiratory infections are another common health issue in ducks. Ducks are very sensitive to damp, dirty, or poorly ventilated environments. These conditions can lead to respiratory problems such as aspergillosis (a fungal infection) or bacterial infections.

To prevent respiratory infections, it is important to keep your ducks' living space clean, dry, and well-ventilated. Avoid overcrowding in their coop, as too many ducks in a small space can lead to poor air circulation, which increases the risk of respiratory problems. Ducks should also have access to fresh air and sunlight. Fresh air helps strengthen their immune systems and keeps them healthy. If you notice signs of respiratory distress in your ducks, such as wheezing, coughing, or nasal discharge, you should consult a veterinarian immediately for proper treatment.

**Parasites**

Ducks can also be affected by parasites. These can be external parasites like mites, lice, and ticks, or internal parasites like worms. Parasites can cause irritation, weight loss, and other health issues for your ducks.

To prevent external parasites, regularly check your ducks for signs such as scratching, feather loss, or visible bugs on their skin. If you spot any parasites, you can treat them with special powders or sprays that are safe for ducks. Internal parasites, like worms, can also cause problems, but they can be prevented by giving your ducks regular deworming treatments.

Keeping the living area clean is also key in preventing parasites. Make sure the coop is free of excess waste, as this can encourage parasite growth. Clean bedding and a well-maintained environment will help reduce the chance of an outbreak.

**General Prevention Tips**

There are several ways to help prevent health issues in your ducks and keep them in top condition. Here are some general tips:

1. Vaccinations: Some vaccines are available for ducks, especially those

that protect against common diseases. Talk to your veterinarian about the available vaccination options for your ducks. Vaccinations can help protect them from serious illnesses.

2. Nutrition: A healthy diet plays a big role in keeping ducks strong and less likely to get sick. Ensure that your ducks have a well-balanced diet and access to clean, fresh water. Proper nutrition supports their immune system, helping them fight off infections and illnesses.

3. Regular Health Checks: It's a good idea to check your ducks regularly for any signs of illness. Make a habit of observing their behavior, appetite, and droppings. If you notice anything unusual, such as changes in behavior or droppings, it may indicate a health problem. Early detection of health issues is important and can prevent bigger problems later on.

## Bathing, Preening, And Grooming

Ducks are naturally clean animals, and grooming is an important part of their daily routine to keep them healthy and comfortable. Bathing, preening, and sometimes even a little help from their owner are all part of their grooming behaviors.

**Bathing**

Ducks need regular access to water so they can bathe and clean their feathers. Bathing is essential for ducks because it helps them keep their feathers in good condition. Water removes dirt, oil, and parasites from their plumage. Ducks love to swim and splash around in ponds, lakes, or small pools. If you have access to a pond or a large pool, that's perfect. If not, you can use a shallow container or kiddie pool to give them a space to bathe in.

The water should always be clean and free from any harmful chemicals, dirt, or debris. Ducks can become very dirty if their water isn't regularly cleaned. When ducks bathe, they often dip into the water, shake off the excess water afterward, and preen their feathers to spread natural oils that help keep them waterproof. This natural oil helps to keep their feathers dry, especially when they swim or when it rains.

In winter, you may need to provide a warmer space for them to bathe, as cold water can be uncomfortable or unsafe for ducks. If you do not have access to a proper swimming area, you can provide them with a shallow dish of water, ensuring they can still clean themselves, but always make sure it's clean and free from contaminants.

**Preening**

Preening is a natural behavior that ducks do to clean and arrange their feathers. Ducks use their beaks to straighten their feathers and remove dirt. They also have a special gland near their tail called the uropygial gland, which produces an oil that they spread over their feathers when they preen. This oil is important because it helps make their feathers waterproof, keeping ducks dry when they swim or when it rains.

Preening is a very important part of a duck's self-care. It helps them stay clean and keeps their feathers in good shape. If you notice that your ducks aren't preening, it could be a sign of a problem. For example, it could mean they don't have enough water to bathe in, or there could be an issue with their oil gland. Make sure your ducks have clean water and enough space to move around so they can preen properly.

**Grooming**

Although ducks are generally good at grooming themselves, there are times when you may need to help them out. Sometimes, ducks can get dirty, or their feathers might get tangled. In these cases, it's okay to step in and assist them gently. You can use a soft brush or comb to carefully remove dirt or debris from their feathers. Be gentle, as ducks can be sensitive, and tugging on their feathers too hard can cause them discomfort.

If your ducks are particularly dirty or have an oil buildup, you can bathe them in lukewarm water. However, avoid using any soaps, shampoos, or detergents, as these can strip their feathers of their natural oils, which are crucial for waterproofing. Simply rinse their feathers in warm water and let them air dry. Make sure to do this gently and calmly to avoid stressing them out.

Ducks may sometimes have difficulty keeping up with their grooming if they are stressed or unwell. If you notice that your ducks are not grooming themselves properly, losing feathers, or showing signs of being overly dirty, it could indicate a health problem. In such cases, it's important to consult with a veterinarian to make sure your ducks are not suffering from an illness or other underlying issue.

**General Care Tips**

In addition to regular bathing and preening, there are a few other things you can do to help your ducks stay healthy:

• Ensure they have plenty of clean water: Access to clean water is crucial for ducks to bathe, drink, and keep their feathers in top condition. Change their water regularly to prevent contamination and bacteria buildup.

• Provide a safe space to preen: Ducks need a quiet, secure place where they can preen without disturbances. This helps them relax and care for themselves properly.

• Check for parasites: While ducks are good at cleaning themselves, they can sometimes pick up parasites like lice or mites. Regularly check your ducks' feathers to make sure they're not infested.

• Give them enough space: Ducks need space to move around and stretch their wings. Crowded conditions can cause stress and lead to grooming issues.

## First Aid And Emergency Care

Accidents can happen at any time, and knowing how to handle them can make a big difference in your duck's health and safety. Having a basic first-aid kit and understanding some simple emergency care steps can help you provide immediate treatment and prevent more serious health problems. Here's what you need to know about first aid and when to seek professional care for your ducks.

**Basic First-Aid Kit for Ducks**

A well-stocked first-aid kit is an essential tool for duck care. Here are some items you should include in your kit:

1. Antiseptic Ointment (safe for animals): This is important for treating cuts or scrapes and preventing infection.

2. Bandages and Gauze: These can be used to cover injuries and protect wounds from dirt and bacteria.

3. Tweezers: Useful for removing splinters, ticks, or other foreign objects

from your duck's skin.

4. Saline Solution or Sterile Water: This is needed to clean wounds before applying any treatment.

5. Hydrocortisone Cream: This can be used for minor irritations, rashes, or bug bites.

6. Thermometer: Helps you check for fever if your duck seems unwell.

By having these basic supplies on hand, you'll be able to handle minor injuries and other issues as they arise.

**Common Treatments for Minor Injuries**

Ducks can sometimes hurt themselves or develop minor health problems that can be treated at home. Here are some common injuries and how to deal with them:

1. Cuts or Scrapes: If your duck has a small cut or scrape, the first thing you should do is clean the wound. Use saline solution or clean, sterile water to gently wash the injury. After cleaning, apply a safe antiseptic ointment to prevent infection. If the wound is in a place where it can be covered, use a clean bandage or gauze to protect it from dirt. Make sure to check the bandage regularly and replace it if needed.

2. Sprained or Broken Limbs: If you suspect that your duck has injured a leg, wing, or other limb, you'll need to act quickly. If you think the injury is a sprain or break, gently immobilize the limb by creating a soft splint to keep it still. Make sure to support the injured area carefully and avoid causing more harm. It's important to contact a veterinarian as soon as possible because broken bones or serious sprains may require professional treatment.

3. Feather Pulling or Bites: Sometimes, ducks can get hurt from pecking or biting, either from other ducks or predators. If your duck has been bitten or has lost feathers due to feather pulling, it's important to clean the wound gently with saline or clean water. Afterward, apply antiseptic ointment to prevent infection. If the injury is serious, you may need to separate the injured duck from the others to stop further damage and give them time to heal.

**When to See a Veterinarian**

While minor injuries and health issues can often be handled at home, there are situations where professional help is needed. You should contact a veterinarian if:

1. Severe Injury: If your duck has a severe injury, such as a deep wound, broken bone, or heavy bleeding, take them to the vet as soon as possible. Serious injuries require immediate attention from a professional to ensure proper treatment and healing.

2. Breathing Problems: If your duck is having trouble breathing or is gasping for air, this could be a sign of a respiratory issue or injury. In such cases, seek veterinary help right away.

3. Signs of Illness: If your duck is showing signs of illness that don't improve with at-home care, such as:

   i. Fever (measured with a thermometer),

   ii. Lethargy (lack of energy or weakness),

   iii. Refusal to eat or drink,

   iv. Changes in behavior, it's time to see a vet. These symptoms could indicate a more serious health problem that requires professional treatment.

4. Ongoing Health Issues: If your duck has a recurring health problem that doesn't improve after a few days of at-home care (like infections, skin problems, or digestive issues), it's important to consult a vet. They can offer the appropriate diagnosis and treatment.

**General First-Aid Tips**

• Stay calm: Ducks can get stressed easily, so it's important to remain calm when handling an injured or sick duck. Speak gently to them and avoid sudden movements.

• Observe behavior: Pay attention to any signs of discomfort or distress. Changes in eating habits, movement, or vocalization can help you notice when something is wrong.

• Prevent infections: Clean wounds carefully and apply antiseptic to prevent infections from developing. Keep the affected area clean and dry, and check regularly for signs of infection, like swelling or pus.

• Provide comfort: Injured ducks may need extra warmth or a quiet place to recover. Keep them in a comfortable, clean area while they heal.

# Chapter 6

## ENRICHMENT AND SOCIALIZATION FOR HAPPY DUCKS

### Creating A Stimulating Environment

Ducks are naturally curious animals that love to explore and stay active. Without enough things to do, they can get bored, which may lead to stress, bad behavior, or even health problems. Creating a stimulating environment for your ducks is important for their mental and physical well-being. It helps keep them happy, healthy, and engaged.

**Duck-Friendly Toys**

Toys may not be something ducks play with in the same way that cats or dogs do, but they still enjoy interacting with different objects. Simple toys and items can provide mental and physical stimulation, which is great for their overall health. Here are some examples of toys and items that ducks enjoy:

1. Balls: Ducks love rolling things around. You can give them rubber balls or large plastic balls that they can push or roll with their beaks. These toys can keep them busy and entertained.

2. Floating Toys: If you have a pond or a pool, you can give your ducks floating toys. Ducks enjoy chasing these toys around or trying to nudge them

out of the water. Floating toys also add an extra level of fun and encourage them to swim.

3. Mirrors: Ducks are often curious about their own reflection. A safe, non-breakable mirror can provide hours of entertainment. Just be sure to securely fasten it to avoid any accidents or injuries.

4. Foraging Materials: Ducks love searching for food, so scattering grains, seeds, or vegetables around their space is a great way to keep them engaged. This mimics natural foraging behaviors and helps keep their minds active. You can even hide some food in different spots to create a fun search for them.

5. Hiding Places: Ducks enjoy exploring areas where they can feel safe and secure. Small boxes or sheltered spots can provide hiding places that encourage exploration. These safe spaces make ducks feel comfortable, while also keeping them curious.

**Mental Stimulation and Enrichment Ideas**

In addition to providing toys, there are many other ways to keep your ducks mentally stimulated and engaged:

1. Foraging and Hiding Food: You can scatter their food around the yard or hide it in different places to encourage your ducks to search for it. Try hiding treats under piles of leaves or in hay bales to create a "treasure hunt." This lets ducks use their natural instincts to search and forage, keeping them active and mentally engaged.

2. Water Features: Ducks are natural swimmers, and they love water. Having access to a pond, kiddie pool, or other water features can provide both physical exercise and mental stimulation. If possible, you can add floating plants, small objects, or even create water obstacles for your ducks to interact with. This adds variety to their day and keeps them entertained for hours.

3. Varied Diets: Ducks enjoy eating different types of food, so changing up their meals can keep them interested. Offer a mix of vegetables, fruits, and grains, and rotate their food each day. For example, one day they can have leafy greens, while the next day they might get some peas or carrots. This variety not only helps them stay mentally engaged but also ensures they get all the necessary nutrients.

**Providing Space for Exploration**

Along with toys and enrichment activities, it's important to give your ducks plenty of space to move around and explore. Ducks need room to dig, forage, and swim to stay happy and healthy. If they are kept in a small, confined space, they may become frustrated and stressed.

When planning a safe area for your ducks, try to provide different textures and areas for them to explore. For example, give them access to grassy areas, dirt patches, or even a small mud puddle. Ducks love to dig, and having various surfaces to explore can keep them entertained.

The more room they have, the more likely they are to engage in natural behaviors. If you have a large, secure outdoor area, your ducks can roam freely, forage for food, and get plenty of exercise. If they're confined to a smaller space, try to make it as varied as possible by adding things like different types of bedding or small areas for them to explore.

## Duck-To-Duck Socialization

Ducks are social animals that thrive in groups. They are happiest when they have companions to interact with. A lone duck can become lonely, stressed, and even depressed without other ducks around. Socializing with fellow ducks is crucial for their emotional well-being, as it helps them feel secure and calm.

**Why Ducks Need Companions**

In the wild, ducks live in flocks, forming strong bonds with one another. These bonds are vital because they help ducks feel safe and relaxed. Ducks often cuddle together, preen each other, and engage in playful behaviors. This social interaction not only helps them stay calm but also strengthens their bond.

When ducks live alone, they can become anxious, which can lead to poor health or even depression. A single duck might feel lost without the company of others. This is why it's so important for ducks to have at least one companion. Ducks in a group or with a friend are much more content and healthier overall. Having a flock also allows them to enjoy activities such as swimming, foraging, and resting together, which is part of their natural behavior.

**How to Introduce New Ducks**

Introducing a new duck to your flock needs to be done carefully to avoid problems like aggression or territorial behavior. Ducks can sometimes be protective of their space, so it's important to follow a few steps to help the new duck fit in smoothly.

1. Quarantine Period: Before bringing a new duck into your flock, keep it in a separate space for a few days. This is a quarantine period where you can check that the new duck is healthy and free from diseases or parasites that could spread to your other ducks. This also gives the new duck time to adjust to its new home.

2. Gradual Introduction: Once the quarantine period is over, start the introduction slowly. Begin by letting the new duck and the existing ducks see each other from a distance. You can place the new duck in a pen or behind a fence where the ducks can see and smell each other but cannot make physical contact yet. This gives them time to get used to one another's presence without the risk of immediate conflict.

3. Supervised Interaction: After the initial separation, you can allow the ducks to meet face-to-face. Make sure to supervise their first few interactions closely. Watch how they behave to ensure there is no aggression. It's normal for ducks to establish a pecking order, meaning they will figure out who is dominant, but this should not turn into fighting. If any fighting occurs, separate the ducks and try again later.

4. Space and Resources: When you introduce a new duck, make sure that there is enough space, food, and water for all of them. If resources like food or water are limited, the ducks might compete, which could lead to stress or fighting. To prevent this, provide multiple areas where the ducks can eat, drink, and rest. This way, they don't have to fight for these basic needs.

Once the new duck has been properly introduced, it should start to bond with the others. Over time, the new duck will become part of the group, and they will learn to live together harmoniously. It's important to be patient during this process, as it may take a few weeks for all the ducks to adjust to the new group dynamic.

**Tips for Successful Duck Socialization**

• Be patient: Ducks are creatures of habit, and it can take time for them to adjust to a new companion. Don't rush the process.

• Observe closely: Watch how the ducks behave when they first meet. Any signs of aggression, such as biting or chasing, should be addressed by separating them and trying again later.

• Ensure safety: Make sure the space where the ducks meet is secure and free from hazards. Avoid putting them in situations where they could hurt themselves or each other.

## Human-Duck Bonding And Interaction

Ducks are intelligent and social animals that can form strong bonds with their human caretakers. Just like with other ducks, they can learn to recognize the people who care for them. Building a good relationship with your ducks will make it easier to handle them and help them stay happy and healthy. Creating trust and having positive interactions are key to developing a bond with your ducks.

**How to Build Trust**

Ducks can be shy, especially if they are not used to being around humans. Building trust takes time, but with consistent and gentle handling, you can develop a strong relationship. Here are some tips to help you build trust with your ducks:

1. Approach Slowly: Ducks can be easily startled, so it's important to approach them calmly and slowly. Avoid sudden movements or loud noises that could frighten them. Give them time to get used to your presence before trying to interact.

2. Offer Treats: Ducks love food, and offering treats is a great way to make them associate you with something positive. You can give them leafy greens, corn, or mealworms. Hold the treat in your hand, and let the duck come to you when it feels comfortable. This creates a sense of trust, as they learn that you bring them something good.

3. Spend Time With Them: Ducks enjoy being around people. Spending time with them helps them get used to your presence. Sit in their area, talk to them softly, or just watch them interact with their environment. This helps them

feel more relaxed and comfortable around you.

4. Gentle Handling: Once your ducks are comfortable with you being around, you can start handling them gently. Always approach them slowly and calmly, and avoid picking them up unless necessary. When handling ducks, it's important to be gentle and not force them to do anything they're not comfortable with. Ducks are sensitive animals, so it's important to treat them with care and respect.

**How to Handle Your Ducks Effectively**

Building a bond with your ducks is essential, but handling them properly is just as important. Ducks can become stressed if they are handled too roughly or inappropriately. Here are some tips on how to handle your ducks in a way that keeps them calm and comfortable:

1. Support Their Bodies: When you need to lift or handle a duck, make sure to support its body properly. Place one hand under its chest and the other under its bottom to keep it secure. This provides support and helps the duck feel safe.

2. Keep Them Calm: Ducks are easily frightened, so it's important to keep them calm when handling them. Speak to them in a soft, reassuring voice and hold them gently. If the duck seems to be struggling or getting stressed, it's best to put them down and give them some space. You can try again later when the duck is feeling more comfortable.

3. Avoid Overhandling: While it's great to spend time with your ducks, it's important not to overhandle them, especially when they're young. Too much handling can be stressful for them and may interfere with their natural behaviors. Ducks need space to roam, explore, and interact with each other. Make sure to balance time spent with them and allowing them to be ducks.

**The Importance of Building a Strong Bond**

Having a good relationship with your ducks makes them easier to care for and helps you provide better care. When ducks trust you, they will be more relaxed and comfortable around you, which makes things like feeding, cleaning, and handling easier. Ducks that feel safe with their human caretakers are also more likely to stay healthy, as they will not be stressed and anxious.

Building a bond with your ducks can also help with their overall happiness.

Ducks that feel loved and cared for are more likely to enjoy interacting with their caretakers and be more social. They will be more comfortable being handled, which can make routine tasks, such as health checks, grooming, and cleaning, easier to manage.

# 7

# Chapter 7

## BREEDING AND RAISING DUCKLINGS

### Understanding Duck Breeding Behavior

Ducks are seasonal breeders, meaning they usually breed at certain times of the year, most commonly in the spring. However, some domesticated ducks may breed throughout the year if the conditions are right. Their breeding behavior is influenced by factors like the time of year, the environment, and the availability of mates. Knowing how ducks breed and their mating habits can help you take better care of them if you plan to breed them.

**Breeding Cycles and Mating Behaviors**

In ducks, it is typically the female (known as the hen) that starts the mating process. When a female duck is ready to mate, she signals this through certain behaviors. One of the ways she shows she's ready is by making soft quacking sounds. She might also dip her head into the water in a behavior known as "dabbling." This signals the male ducks (drakes) that she is available for mating.

Once the male sees these signals, he will start courting the female. He might follow her around, try to impress her by offering food, or perform a special behavior called "head bobbing," where he rapidly bobs his head up and down. This is his way of showing interest in her.

If the female duck is receptive, she will allow the male to approach her. Mating often takes place in or near water, as ducks are water-loving animals. However, it is also possible for mating to occur on land. After mating, the female duck will begin laying eggs.

**Egg-Laying Habits**

Ducks lay one egg per day, typically in the morning. The number of eggs in a clutch (the total number of eggs laid) can vary depending on the breed of duck. Most ducks lay between 8 and 15 eggs in one batch. After the female has finished laying all of her eggs, she will start the process of incubating them. Incubation is when the female stays on the nest to keep the eggs warm, as warmth is essential for the eggs to develop properly.

During the incubation period, the female will rarely leave the nest. She may leave for short periods to eat, drink, or bathe, but most of the time, she stays on the eggs. Some ducks are very attentive to their eggs and will sit on them carefully, while others may need assistance if they are not taking good care of the nest.

The incubation period for duck eggs usually lasts about 28 days, depending on the breed. During this time, the female keeps the eggs warm with her body heat and turns them regularly to ensure even development. Once the eggs are ready to hatch, the ducklings will break through the eggshells and begin their journey into the world.

**Creating a Safe Nesting Environment**

If you are planning to breed your ducks, it's important to make sure they have a good place to lay and incubate their eggs. Female ducks prefer a quiet and safe area to nest. They like a secluded spot where they can feel secure. You can help by providing them with a comfortable space in a quiet area away from too much noise or activity. A nest with soft bedding, such as straw, feathers, or grass, will make the female feel more at ease while laying her eggs.

It's also important to provide some protection for the nest to ensure the eggs and the female are safe from predators. Ducks are very protective of their nests, so giving them a secure and private place will help them feel more comfortable and encourage them to incubate the eggs properly.

## Incubating Eggs Vs. Natural Hatching

When it comes to hatching duck eggs, you have two main choices: you can either let the female duck (hen) incubate them naturally, or you can use an incubator to hatch the eggs yourself. Each method has its advantages, and the right choice will depend on your situation.

**Natural Hatching**

In nature, female ducks (hens) are very capable of incubating their eggs themselves. If the hen is healthy and has a proper place to nest, she will usually handle the incubation process without any help. The incubation period for duck eggs is about 28 days, although this can vary slightly depending on the breed.

During incubation, the female sits on her eggs and uses her body heat to keep them warm. She doesn't need any assistance with this process, but there are a few things you can do to help her succeed.

First, make sure she has a safe, quiet area to incubate her eggs. Ducks prefer a secluded, stress-free place where they can focus on keeping their eggs warm. Keep other animals away from her nesting area to reduce any potential stress or disturbance.

While incubating, the female will leave the nest occasionally to eat, drink, or bathe. It's important to ensure she has easy access to food and fresh water during these times. If she feels safe and well cared for, she will return to the nest to continue incubating the eggs.

If you choose to let the female duck incubate the eggs naturally, make sure she's comfortable, healthy, and free from distractions. She will take care of the rest on her own.

**Incubating Eggs in an Incubator**

If you decide to incubate the eggs yourself, or if the female duck is not properly incubating them, you can use an incubator. Incubators allow you to control the temperature and humidity, which is very important for the development of the duck embryos. They can also ensure that the eggs are turned regularly, which is something the female would do naturally by shifting around on the nest.

Here's how to incubate duck eggs using an incubator:

1. Set the Temperature and Humidity: The incubator needs to be set to the right temperature and humidity for the eggs to develop. The temperature should be about 99.5°F (37.5°C), and the humidity should be around 50-55%. As the eggs near hatching, you should increase the humidity to 65-70% to help the ducklings hatch more easily.

2. Turn the Eggs Regularly: Duck eggs need to be turned several times a day to keep the embryos from sticking to the shell. If your incubator has an automatic turner, it will do this for you. If not, you will need to turn the eggs by hand at least three times a day. Regular turning is crucial for the healthy development of the ducklings inside the eggs.

3. Monitor the Eggs: Check the incubator daily to make sure the temperature and humidity levels are stable. Also, make sure the eggs are clean and dry. Keeping the incubator clean is important to prevent any bacteria or mold from developing.

The incubation period for duck eggs is typically 28 days, but it can vary depending on the breed of duck. During the last few days of incubation, you should stop turning the eggs and increase the humidity to help the ducklings break through the shells.

As the eggs approach the end of the incubation period, you might start hearing sounds from inside the eggs. The ducklings begin "pipping" — this is when they start cracking the eggshell. Once the eggs are cracked, the ducklings will usually fully emerge on their own.

**Deciding Between Natural and Artificial Incubation**

Both methods of hatching, natural and artificial, can be successful, but each has its pros and cons.

Natural hatching is great because the female duck knows exactly what to do. She is very experienced in keeping the eggs warm and turning them as needed. It also means you don't have to worry about managing an incubator or checking the eggs every day.

However, there are some potential downsides to natural hatching. If the female is not taking good care of the eggs, or if there are too many distractions or dangers in her environment, it can affect the success rate. In some cases, a duck might not be a good sitter and could abandon her eggs, leaving them to go cold.

Using an incubator gives you more control over the process. You can ensure the eggs are kept at the right temperature and humidity, and you can also monitor them closely for any problems. Incubators are particularly useful if you need to hatch eggs without a mother duck, or if the female is not providing good care for her eggs.

However, incubating eggs yourself requires more attention and effort. You need to monitor the temperature and humidity levels, make sure the eggs are being turned, and check them regularly.

## Duckling Care And Growth Stages

Once your duck eggs have hatched, it's time to start caring for the little ducklings. Ducklings are delicate and require specific care to grow into strong and healthy adult ducks. They need the right food, warmth, safety, and space to grow properly. Here's everything you need to know about caring for your ducklings during their early growth stages.

**Feeding Ducklings**

When ducklings first hatch, they can survive for 24 to 48 hours on the yolk sac inside their bodies. This means they don't need food immediately after hatching. However, after this time, they will need to start eating. It is important to feed them the right food to ensure they grow strong and healthy.

You should feed your ducklings a special duckling starter feed that's designed for their nutritional needs. This feed should contain 18-20% protein, which helps them grow quickly. Make sure the feed does not have any medicated ingredients meant for other types of poultry, as these can be harmful to ducklings.

Along with duckling feed, you can offer small amounts of finely chopped vegetables like lettuce or peas. However, these should only be treats, and the main portion of their diet should be the duckling starter feed.

Ducklings also need fresh water at all times. They drink often and can make a mess with the water, so be sure to provide a shallow container that allows them to dip their beaks in but is not deep enough for them to drown. Always keep the water clean and fresh for the ducklings to drink.

**Warmth and Housing**

Ducklings need warmth, especially during their first few weeks, as they are not able to regulate their body temperature. This is why it's important to provide a heat source for them. A heat lamp or a brooder (a small, warm enclosure) is ideal for keeping them warm.

For the first week, the temperature should be kept at 90°F (32°C). After that, you can gradually lower the temperature by 5°F each week until they have developed their adult feathers and can handle normal temperatures. By the time they are around 6 weeks old, they will be able to tolerate cooler temperatures.

In addition to warmth, ducklings need a clean, dry space to sleep and rest. A small brooder with bedding such as straw or wood shavings works well. Make sure the bedding is dry and free from contaminants like mold or bacteria, which could harm the ducklings. It's also important to change the bedding regularly to keep the area clean.

**Safety for Ducklings**

Ducklings are vulnerable to predators, so it's important to keep them safe in a secure environment. If you are keeping your ducklings outside, make sure their enclosure is well-protected with sturdy fencing to keep out any potential threats like raccoons, foxes, or other animals that may harm them.

Besides physical protection from predators, ducklings also need a calm and quiet environment. They can become frightened by loud noises or sudden movements, so try to keep their living area peaceful. Ducklings are very social animals, so it's also important to keep them with other ducklings for companionship. Being with other ducklings will help them feel secure and less stressed.

**Growth Stages**

Ducklings grow quickly, and in just 6 to 8 weeks, they will start to develop adult feathers. As they grow, they will become more independent and start exploring their surroundings. During this time, it's important to continue providing them with a balanced diet to support their growth.

As your ducklings get older, you can gradually start transitioning them from the brooder to a larger outdoor enclosure. This allows them to explore more and learn how to be independent, but they will still need your supervision until they are fully matured and able to care for themselves.

By the time your ducklings are around 8 weeks old, they will be much more self-sufficient. They will have developed most of their adult feathers, and you can start introducing them to a larger, safer outdoor environment where they can swim, forage, and continue their development.

# 8

# Chapter 8

## TRAINING YOUR DUCK

### Basic Commands And Tricks

Training your duck to follow simple commands can be a fun and rewarding way to bond with them. Ducks are smart animals and can learn to respond to different cues, but remember that their attention span is shorter than that of other pets, like dogs. Training a duck takes patience, consistency, and a gentle approach. Here are a few basic commands and tricks that you can teach your duck.

**Teaching Ducks to Come**

One of the first things you might want to teach your duck is the "come" command. This command is helpful when you want to call your duck back into their enclosure or bring them inside. Here's how you can train your duck to come when called:

1. Start with treats: Ducks love food, so use their favorite treats to get their attention. Small pieces of peas, leafy greens, or corn work great.

2. Call their name: Stand a few feet away from your duck and call its name in a happy, excited voice. Hold out the treat to get their attention.

3. Reward the behavior: When the duck comes to you, immediately give

them the treat and praise them. This will help your duck connect coming to you with a positive reward.

4. Repeat regularly: Practice this several times a day. As your duck gets better at the command, increase the distance between you and your duck. Over time, they will learn to come when you call them.

**Teaching Ducks to Sit**

Teaching a duck to sit on command can be more challenging than other pets, but it is possible with patience. Ducks naturally sit or squat when they rest, so they are familiar with this behavior. Here's a method you can try:

1. Get the duck's attention: Hold a treat in your hand and make sure your duck can see it.

2. Encourage the sit position: Slowly lower the treat toward the ground, making the duck bend down to reach it. This will encourage the duck to squat or sit.

3. Reward and praise: When the duck sits, immediately give them the treat and praise them for sitting. Positive reinforcement is key.

4. Practice consistently: Repeat this several times. Over time, your duck may begin to sit on command. Patience is important, and some ducks may take longer than others to learn this trick.

**Teaching Ducks to Respond to Their Name**

Ducks are social animals and can learn to recognize their names, much like dogs or cats. Teaching your duck to respond to its name can be useful for training and bonding. Here's how you can do it:

1. Choose a short, distinct name: Ducks respond best to short names that have clear sounds. Pick a simple name like "Daisy," "Bill," or another name that's easy to say.

2. Use the name consistently: Every time you interact with your duck, say its name. Use it when you feed them, call them, or simply talk to them.

3. Give rewards: Whenever your duck turns to look at you or responds when you say their name, reward them with a treat and praise them. This helps your duck link their name with something positive.

4. Repeat the process: The more often you use the name and reward your duck, the faster they will learn to recognize it and respond. Be patient and

keep practicing, as this will help reinforce the connection between their name and the reward.

**General Tips for Training Ducks**

• Be patient: Ducks take time to learn commands. Don't expect them to get it right away. If you stay calm and patient, they will eventually learn.

• Use positive reinforcement: Ducks respond best to rewards like treats and praise. Always reward them immediately after they perform the behavior you want.

• Keep training sessions short: Ducks have shorter attention spans than other pets, so keep training sessions brief and fun. About 5-10 minutes per session is enough.

• Make it fun: Training should be a positive experience for both you and your duck. Keep things light and enjoyable so your duck stays interested.

## Potty Training Ducks

Potty training ducks might seem unusual, but it's possible, especially if you have a house duck or a duck that spends a lot of time indoors. Ducks have natural bathroom habits, and they often go to the bathroom in specific spots, which you can use to your advantage when training them. Here's a guide to potty training ducks and the pros and cons of the process.

**Pros and Cons of Potty Training Ducks**

**Pros:**

• Cleaner Environment: One of the biggest benefits of potty training your duck is that it helps keep your home cleaner. By training your duck to use a designated potty area, you can avoid accidents and reduce the amount of waste in your home.

• Healthier Space: Training your duck to relieve itself in a specific place makes cleaning easier and helps maintain a more hygienic environment in your living space.

**Cons:**

• Inconsistency: Ducks may not always use their designated potty spot, especially if they are young, nervous, or distracted. It can take some time for them to get into the routine, and they might still have accidents now and then.

• Frequent Cleaning: Even with potty training, ducks can produce a lot of waste, so you will need to clean their potty area often. It can be time-consuming to keep their area tidy.

**How to Potty Train Ducks**

1. Choose a Designated Spot The first step in potty training your duck is to pick a specific area where you want them to go. Ducks tend to relieve themselves after they eat or when they wake up, so these are good times to encourage them to use their potty area. You can use a small litter box or an area with absorbent bedding like straw or pine shavings. Ducks enjoy having a clean, soft space to go to the bathroom, so make it comfortable for them.

2. Place the Duck in the Spot Once you've chosen the spot, you can start training by placing the duck in the designated area. Pay attention to their behavior—if you notice them squatting or looking like they need to go, gently guide them to the potty area. Ducks often give small signs when they need to relieve themselves, such as walking away from where they were or pausing to look around. When your duck uses the potty area correctly, immediately reward them with a treat or praise. Positive reinforcement will help them connect going to the bathroom in that spot with something good.

3. Be Consistent and Patient Potty training takes time, so it's important to be consistent. Repeat the process regularly, especially after meals or when your duck wakes up, as these are common times for bathroom breaks. Every time your duck uses the potty area correctly, reward them with a treat or praise. Over time, your duck will start to understand that this is the place to go. Be patient and remember that it may take some time for your duck to get the hang of it.

4. Use Absorbent Bedding Ducks like to have a clean area to go to the bathroom, so make sure the designated potty spot has comfortable bedding. You can use absorbent materials like straw, pine shavings, or even puppy pads in the potty area. These materials help absorb moisture and make cleaning easier. Clean the area regularly to keep it fresh and comfortable for your duck.

**Tips for Success**

• Watch for Signs: Ducks often go to the bathroom after eating or when they wake up. Watch for signs that they need to go, such as squatting or walking away from where they were. This is a good time to guide them to the potty area.

· Stay Calm: If your duck has an accident or doesn't use the potty area at first, don't get frustrated. Potty training can take time, and accidents are part of the process.

· Repeat Often: The more often you guide your duck to the potty area, the faster they will learn. Make the process a regular part of your day.

· Keep it Clean: Regularly clean the potty area to avoid smells and keep it a pleasant space for your duck. Ducks prefer a clean place to go to the bathroom, and keeping the area tidy helps encourage them to use it.

## Reward-Based Training

The most effective way to train your duck is through reward-based training. Ducks are very food-motivated, meaning they respond well to treats as rewards for good behavior. Using positive reinforcement, like treats and praise, helps your duck understand what behaviors you want them to repeat. This method is enjoyable for both you and your duck and can lead to a well-behaved and trained pet.

**Using Treats and Positive Reinforcement**

To train your duck using treats, follow these steps:

1. Choose the Right Treats Ducks love different types of food, and offering the right treats can be very effective in training. Some popular treats for ducks include peas, corn, and leafy greens like lettuce or spinach. These foods are nutritious and loved by ducks. However, it's important to give treats in moderation, as overfeeding can cause health problems. Keep treats as an occasional reward rather than a regular part of their diet to avoid making your duck too dependent on them.

2. Timing is Important For reward-based training to be successful, you need to give the treat at the right moment. The key is to reward your duck immediately after they do what you want. This helps your duck understand that the action they just performed is the reason for the reward. For example,

if you're training your duck to come when called, as soon as the duck reaches you, give them the treat right away. The quicker you reward them, the stronger the connection will be between the action and the reward.

3. Use Consistent Cues Ducks need consistency to understand what you want them to do. Always use the same words, hand gestures, and tone of voice for each command. For example, if you want your duck to come to you, always say the same word, like "come" or their name. If you use different words or a different tone each time, it will confuse the duck and make training harder. Repeating the same cues will help your duck quickly learn and associate the behavior with the specific command.

4. Be Patient Ducks are not as quick to learn as some other animals, and they have shorter attention spans. It's important to keep training sessions short, around 5 to 10 minutes at a time, to avoid overwhelming or frustrating your duck. If a session goes on too long, your duck might lose interest and stop focusing on the training. Ending the session while your duck is still engaged and eager to participate is a good way to make them look forward to the next training session. Be patient with your duck, as it may take several sessions before they fully grasp the command or behavior.

5. Gradually Reduce the Treats At the beginning of training, treats are an important way to motivate your duck. However, once your duck starts to understand the commands and behaviors, you can begin to reduce the number of treats you give. Instead of giving a treat every time, try giving a treat only occasionally and use praise as a reward instead. Ducks also enjoy verbal praise, so saying things like "good job!" or "well done!" in a happy tone can be just as effective as a treat. This will help your duck learn to perform the behavior even when there are no treats involved, making the training more lasting.

**Additional Tips for Successful Training**

• Be Clear and Simple: Keep your commands simple and straightforward. Ducks don't need complicated instructions, so use short words and clear signals.

• Consistency is Key: Practice commands regularly, and always reward your duck when they perform the desired behavior. The more you reinforce positive behavior, the more likely your duck will repeat it.

- Make Training Fun: Training should be enjoyable for both you and your duck. If your duck enjoys the process, they will be more motivated to learn. Keep the sessions light and fun, using their favorite treats to keep them engaged.

**9**

# Chapter 9

## SEASONAL CARE AND ADAPTING TO WEATHER

### Summer Care Tips

Summer can be a fun time for ducks since they love swimming and spending time outdoors. However, hot weather can also be dangerous for them. Heat can lead to dehydration and overheating, so it's important to take steps to keep your ducks cool and safe. Here are some helpful tips for caring for your ducks in the summer heat.

**Preventing Overheating**

Ducks, like many animals, can struggle in hot weather. Their thick feathers can trap heat, and while they enjoy being outside, they need help staying cool during high temperatures. Here's how you can protect them from overheating:

1. Provide Plenty of Water

Ducks need a lot of water, especially during hot weather. Without enough water, they can become dehydrated very quickly. Make sure they always have access to fresh, cool water throughout the day. It's a good idea to provide water sources like a kiddie pool or a small pond where they can swim and cool off. Swimming is one of their favorite activities, and it helps them regulate their body temperature.

2. Ensure Access to Shade

Ducks need shade to escape the sun's heat. In hot weather, make sure they have a shady spot where they can relax and cool down. You can set up a simple shade structure, like a tarp or umbrella, or let them use natural shade from trees or bushes. This will give them a break from the heat and keep them comfortable.

3. Avoid the Hottest Hours of the Day

The hottest part of the day is usually between noon and 3 p.m. If possible, try to keep your ducks indoors or in a cool area during these hours. If they must stay outside, make sure they have plenty of water and access to shaded areas to help them stay cool.

Water Safety

Ducks love to swim, and summer is the best time for them to enjoy water. However, you should make sure that their swimming areas are safe and clean to prevent any health issues.

1. Clean Swimming Areas

If your ducks have access to a pond, kiddie pool, or other water sources, it's important to keep the water clean. Dirty water can lead to illness or infections in ducks. Be sure to regularly clean any pools or ponds they use to prevent bacteria and parasites from growing.

2. Supervised Swimming

If your ducks are swimming in deep water, make sure to keep an eye on them. Ducks can tire quickly in deep water, so it's important to make sure they have places to rest in shallow areas. You can add shallow areas to a pond or provide small shallow pools where the ducks can cool off safely.

3. Avoid Stagnant Water

Stagnant water, or water that doesn't move, can be a breeding ground for harmful bacteria and parasites. Make sure that any water your ducks use is clean and moving. If you have a pond, ensure it's properly filtered or refreshed regularly to keep it safe for your ducks.

**Protecting from Bugs and Pests**

Summer also brings more bugs and pests like mosquitoes, flies, and mites, which can bother your ducks or make them sick. Here's how to protect them from pests:

1. Provide a Safe Sleeping Area

Make sure your ducks sleep in a clean, dry area that is free from mosquitoes and other insects. A good sleeping area will help keep your ducks comfortable at night. You can also use natural insect repellents like citronella or garlic to keep bugs away. Make sure their sleeping area is well-ventilated and protected from pests.

2. Regularly Check for Pests

It's important to inspect your ducks regularly for pests like mites, lice, or fleas, which are more common in warm weather. If you notice any signs of irritation, scratching, or unusual behavior, check for pests. Keeping your ducks clean and grooming them regularly can also help prevent infestations.

**Other Summer Tips**

1. Avoid Overfeeding

During hot weather, ducks can become less active. You might be tempted to feed them more to keep them full, but it's important not to overfeed them. Ducks can gain weight quickly, especially in the summer when they aren't as active. Offer a balanced diet with plenty of fresh greens, and avoid giving them too many high-calorie treats.

2. Keep Their Enclosure Clean

Keeping your ducks' living area clean is especially important in the summer when they spend more time outside. Regularly clean their coop and any water sources to reduce the risk of illness. Provide fresh bedding like straw or wood shavings to keep their area dry and comfortable.

## Winter Care Tips

Winter can be a tough time for ducks, as cold temperatures and harsh weather conditions present challenges for their well-being. Ducks have a natural ability to tolerate cold, but they still need extra care and attention to stay safe and healthy during the winter months. Here are some important tips for keeping your ducks comfortable in the winter.

**Housing and Insulation**

Providing a warm, dry shelter is the first step to protecting your ducks in the winter. While ducks can handle cold weather, they need a safe space to sleep and stay warm when the temperatures drop.

1. Insulate Their Shelter

Ducks need a comfortable place to sleep, especially during extreme cold. Make sure their coop or shelter is insulated properly to keep the cold wind out. You can line the floor with straw or hay, which helps trap heat and keeps the shelter warmer. This bedding also absorbs waste, which helps keep the area cleaner and drier.

2. Provide Plenty of Bedding

Thick bedding, like straw, is essential for keeping your ducks warm. It will not only keep them cozy but also help absorb waste and moisture, which prevents the shelter from becoming damp and cold. Change the bedding regularly to maintain a clean environment.

3. Protect From Drafts

Drafts can make your ducks' shelter much colder, so it's important to block any cold air from entering. You can use tarps, plastic sheeting, or other weatherproof barriers to seal any gaps or openings in their housing. This will create a warmer, safer environment for them during winter.

**Keeping Water Unfrozen**

Ducks need access to fresh water for drinking and cleaning their feathers. During winter, one of the biggest challenges is keeping their water from freezing, as they cannot drink or bathe in frozen water.

1. Use Heated Water Bowls

To prevent water from freezing, you can use a heated water bowl or a de-icer. These devices are safe and designed to keep the water from freezing during the cold winter months. By maintaining a steady supply of liquid water, your ducks can stay hydrated and healthy.

2. Change Water Frequently

Even with a heated water bowl, it's important to check the water regularly. Sometimes, water can still freeze if the temperatures are low enough or become contaminated with droppings or debris. Make sure to clean and change the water frequently to ensure your ducks always have access to fresh water.

3. Provide Smaller, Shallow Containers

Sometimes, smaller water containers can be easier to manage in freezing weather. They are quicker to clean and refill, and they may be less likely to freeze completely. Just be sure to change the water often, so your ducks have enough to drink and clean themselves.

**Preventing Frostbite**

Frostbite is a serious risk for ducks, especially in very cold weather. Their feet and combs are most vulnerable to frostbite, so it's important to take precautions to protect them.

1. Avoid Cold, Wet Conditions

Ducks can handle the cold, but they need to keep their feet dry to avoid frostbite. Wet conditions, especially during winter, can cause their feet to freeze. Make sure your ducks have dry areas to walk and rest in. If their bedding or outdoor space gets wet, dry it out as soon as possible to reduce the risk of frostbite.

2. Use Petroleum Jelly or Duck-Safe Ointment

To help protect your ducks' feet and combs from frostbite, you can apply a thin layer of petroleum jelly or a special duck-safe ointment. These products create a barrier that helps protect against cold wind and freezing temperatures. Apply the ointment regularly, especially during very cold weather.

3. Monitor for Signs of Frostbite

Check your ducks regularly for signs of frostbite, particularly on their feet and combs. Signs of frostbite include blackened or swollen areas on their feet, comb, or wattles. If you notice these signs, warm up the affected area gently. You can use lukewarm water or a warm cloth to help thaw frozen areas. If the frostbite seems severe, consult a veterinarian for advice and treatment.

**Additional Winter Tips**

1. Keep Ducks Active

Ducks still need exercise during the winter months. If it's safe to do so, allow them some time to move around outdoors. Be sure to provide a dry, non-slippery surface for them to walk on. Avoid letting them walk on ice, as it can cause injury.

2. Provide Extra Food

Ducks may need extra food during the winter to help them maintain their energy. Offer them a balanced diet that includes grains, seeds, and fresh greens. You can also provide treats like cracked corn, which gives them extra warmth and energy.

## Adapting To Changing Seasons

As the seasons change, so do the needs of your ducks. It's important to adjust your ducks' care routines to make sure they stay healthy, comfortable, and safe throughout the year. Whether it's adjusting their diet, housing, or exercise routine, here's how to take care of your ducks in each season.

**Adjusting Their Diet**

Ducks' dietary needs can change with the seasons. It's important to provide the right amount of food to match the temperature and the duck's activity level.

1. Summer Diet

In warmer months, ducks tend to be more active and may forage more. They enjoy exploring and looking for food outdoors, so they might need slightly less food than in the winter. However, they still need a steady supply of fresh greens and high-quality duck feed to meet their nutritional needs. Make sure they have plenty of water, as they drink more during the summer to stay hydrated and cool. Offer vegetables like lettuce, peas, and corn to supplement their diet, but avoid overfeeding to prevent weight gain.

2. Winter Diet

During colder months, ducks require more calories to help them stay warm. Their bodies burn more energy in the cold, so it's important to adjust their diet to meet their increased energy needs. You can add high-energy foods like cracked corn or oats to their meals. These foods provide extra warmth and help your ducks stay strong in the cold weather. Be sure to continue providing plenty of fresh vegetables and grains, which help balance their diet and support their overall health.

**Adjusting Their Housing**

The housing your ducks live in should be adapted to suit the weather conditions of each season.

1. Summer Housing

In the summer, it's important to provide your ducks with a cool and comfortable place to sleep. Make sure their housing is well-ventilated, as this helps keep the area cooler and more breathable during hot weather. Shade is also crucial to protect them from the sun's direct heat. You can use trees, tarps, or shade structures to create cool resting areas. Ensure that they always have access to fresh, cool water to drink and bathe in.

2. Winter Housing

When winter comes, your ducks will need extra protection from the cold. Insulate their shelter to keep the cold out and to trap heat inside. You can use materials like straw, hay, or blankets to line the shelter and provide extra warmth. Make sure there are no drafts or cold air entering their housing. The bedding in their shelter should be thick and dry to help keep them comfortable during freezing temperatures. Adding extra layers of bedding and ensuring the shelter is windproof will help keep your ducks warm and safe.

**Adjusting Their Exercise Routine**

Ducks need exercise and mental stimulation all year long, but how you provide this exercise may change depending on the season.

1. Summer Exercise

In the warmer months, ducks love spending time outdoors, swimming in water, and foraging for food. This natural behavior is great for their physical and mental health, so make sure they have plenty of space to roam. A pond or kiddie pool can provide them with the opportunity to swim and splash around. If possible, let them free-range in a safe, enclosed area so they can explore and find food, which also helps keep them active and happy.

2. Winter Exercise

While ducks still need exercise in the winter, outdoor activities may be limited due to colder weather. If there is snow or ice, your ducks might not be able to swim or roam as freely. You can still provide them with indoor playtime or smaller, sheltered spaces where they can move around. Set up an area with straw or hay where they can dig, forage, and explore. You can also provide them with enrichment activities like treats hidden in their bedding, which

CHAPTER 9

encourages them to move and stay active even when it's too cold to go outside.

# 10

## Chapter 10

## COMMON QUESTIONS AND TROUBLESHOOTING

### Managing Noise And Behavioral Issues

Ducks are social animals, and while they can be very entertaining, they can also be quite noisy and exhibit certain behavioral issues, especially during mating season or if they are stressed. Understanding how to manage these behaviors will help ensure a peaceful and happy environment for both you and your ducks. Here are some tips to address common concerns like loud quacking, aggression, and other behavioral issues.

**Handling Loud Quacking**

Loud quacking is one of the most common concerns for duck owners. Ducks can quack loudly, especially early in the morning, when they are excited, or when they want attention. While quacking is natural for ducks, there are ways to manage the noise.

1. Provide Stimulation and Enrichment

Ducks often quack when they are bored or seeking attention. To prevent this, try offering more activities that keep them engaged. You can provide toys, make foraging activities available, or even set up a kiddie pool for water play. These activities help keep your ducks mentally and physically stimulated, which can reduce the desire to quack for attention.

2. Create a Routine

Ducks thrive on routine, and when they know what to expect, they tend to feel more relaxed. For example, feeding your ducks at the same time every day can help reduce anxious quacking. Knowing when to expect food or social time makes ducks feel secure and less likely to make noise unnecessarily.

3. Limit Stimuli

Ducks may become more vocal when they see other animals or people outside their living space. If possible, try to place their housing in a quieter, more secluded area. This can help reduce the excitement that comes from seeing movement outside, which often triggers loud quacking.

**Addressing Aggression**

Aggression is another common behavioral issue in ducks. It can happen for a variety of reasons, including territorial behavior, dominance, or stress. Here's how to handle aggression in ducks:

1. Socialize Ducks Early

Ducks are social animals, and they usually get along well with others. However, aggression can arise if they aren't introduced to each other properly. When adding new ducks to your flock, do so gradually and under controlled conditions. This helps the ducks get used to each other in a safe way, reducing the chances of fighting or aggression.

2. Provide Enough Space

Crowding can lead to stress, which in turn can cause aggression. If your ducks feel cramped or threatened, they may fight or act aggressively. Make sure they have plenty of space to roam and explore. If you have multiple ducks, ensure they have room to establish their own territories to prevent fights over space.

3. Monitor During Breeding Season

Ducks can become more territorial and aggressive during the breeding season. Males, in particular, can show increased aggression as they compete for mates. If aggression becomes a problem, try separating the aggressive duck temporarily. Once the situation calms down, you can reintroduce the ducks to each other gradually.

**Managing Other Behavioral Issues**

In addition to noise and aggression, ducks may display other behavioral problems, such as feather plucking or excessive restlessness. Here's how to manage these issues:

1. Provide a Balanced Environment

Ducks need a mix of social interaction, space to forage, and time to relax. If they don't get enough of any of these, they may become stressed or bored, which can lead to unwanted behaviors. Make sure your ducks have plenty of opportunities to forage for food, as this helps them stay busy and entertained. It's also important for them to have some quiet time, especially in a calm, safe space where they can rest.

2. Check for Health Issues

Sometimes, behavioral problems in ducks are linked to health issues. If a duck is acting unusually aggressive, lethargic, or restless, it could be a sign of illness or discomfort. If you notice any changes in your duck's behavior that seem out of the ordinary, it's a good idea to consult a veterinarian. Health concerns like parasites, injuries, or infections can lead to changes in behavior, so it's important to rule out medical issues.

## Dealing With Messes And Cleaning Routines

Ducks are known to be messy, but with the right cleaning routine, it's easy to manage their mess and keep their living space clean. A clean environment is important not only for your ducks' comfort but also for their health. Regular cleaning helps prevent diseases, parasites, and unpleasant odors, ensuring that your ducks stay happy and healthy.

**Efficient Cleaning Methods**

To keep your ducks' living area clean, there are several effective cleaning methods to follow. Here's a step-by-step guide:

1. Clean Their Water Regularly

Ducks can make a mess with their water. They splash around, dip their beaks, and sometimes even swim in it. This means that their water can get dirty quickly. To prevent your ducks from drinking contaminated water, you should clean and change it at least once a day, or more often if they have a large water source like a pond. Use water containers that are easy to clean, such as plastic or metal bowls. This will make it simpler to maintain fresh water for your ducks.

2. Use Bedding to Absorb Waste

Bedding is essential for keeping the coop dry and odor-free. Cover the floor of their coop with absorbent materials like straw, hay, or wood shavings. These materials soak up moisture and waste, which helps keep the living space clean. Be sure to replace the bedding regularly, ideally once a week, but more often if it becomes soiled. This will help keep the area dry and reduce bad smells.

3. Spot Clean Daily

In addition to changing the bedding, make it a habit to spot clean your ducks' living area every day. Look for any visible waste or soiled areas and clean them up quickly. This daily cleaning helps prevent the buildup of bacteria and makes the weekly deep cleaning process much easier. By cleaning up as you go, you'll avoid unpleasant odors and ensure that your ducks' space remains comfortable.

4. Deep Clean Weekly

A deeper clean is necessary once a week to maintain a hygienic environment. Remove all the bedding from the coop, and clean the floors and walls with a mild disinfectant. Be sure to clean all the areas your ducks frequent, including feeders, water bowls, and any toys or accessories they use. After cleaning, replace the bedding with fresh materials to keep the coop dry and cozy. This thorough cleaning helps prevent germs and parasites from spreading and keeps your ducks healthy.

**Managing Outdoor Messes**

If your ducks have access to an outdoor run or roam freely in your yard or garden, you may find that they leave droppings around. While this is completely natural, it can become overwhelming, especially in smaller spaces. Here are a few ways to manage messes outdoors:

1. Provide a Designated Bathroom Area

One way to make cleaning easier is to designate a specific area for your ducks to use as their bathroom. You can create a small fenced-off area with bedding where they can go to the bathroom. This helps keep the mess concentrated in one spot and makes it easier for you to clean up. Ducks are creatures of habit, so they may start to prefer this designated area over other parts of the yard.

2. Use a Composting System

Duck droppings are actually a great addition to a compost pile. If you have a garden, you can compost duck waste to fertilize your plants. However, it's important to age the droppings properly before adding them to your compost pile, as fresh duck manure can be too strong for plants. Make sure your composting area is separate from your ducks' living spaces and that the compost is kept at the proper temperature and moisture level to break down safely. This way, you can recycle the mess in a productive way while keeping the yard clean.

**General Tips for Cleanliness**

Here are a few more general tips to help keep your ducks' living environment clean and fresh:

1. Clean Regularly

Consistency is key to maintaining a clean space for your ducks. Make a cleaning schedule that includes daily spot cleaning, weekly deep cleaning, and regular water changes. This will help prevent problems before they arise and keep your ducks healthy and comfortable.

2. Use Natural Cleaners

When cleaning your ducks' space, avoid harsh chemicals, which can be harmful to them. Instead, use natural cleaners or mild soap and water. These are safer for your ducks and still effective at keeping their space clean.

3. Check for Pests

Regularly inspect your ducks' living space for signs of pests like mites, lice, or fleas. If you spot any, take action immediately to remove them. Keeping the area clean and dry will help discourage pests from settling in.

Made in the USA
Columbia, SC
28 May 2025

58603041R00041